**Stepping into Standards
Theme Series**

Rocks and Minerals

Written by
Vicky Shiotsu

Editor: Sheri Rous
Illustrator: Jenny Campbell
Cover Illustrators: Darcy Tom and Kimberly Schamber
Designer: Moonhee Pak
Cover Designer: Moonhee Pak
Art Director: Tom Cochrane
Project Director: Carolea Williams

Table of Contents

INTRODUCTION 3

GETTING STARTED

How to Use This Book 4
Meeting Standards 6
Introducing . . . Rocks and Minerals 8
Rocks and Minerals Pretest 9
What Do You Know? KWL Chart 10
Rocks and Minerals—Reading Comprehension Test 11

LANGUAGE ARTS

Our Rocky Earth 13
Layers of the Earth 14
What Are Rocks? 15
Erupting Volcanoes 16
Rock Particles 17
Granite vs. Gneiss 18
Words to Know 18
Verb Ending Challenge 19
Antonym and Synonym Search 20
Rock Letter 20
Describe a Rock 21
If You Find a Rock 22
A New Ending for Sylvester 23
A Magic Pebble 23

MATH

Weigh and Compare 31
Mount Rushmore—A Towering Memorial 32
Rocks for Sale 33
Shopping for Gemstones 34
Gemstone Geometry 35
Birthday Survey 36
How Many Pebbles? 37
A Game of Chance 37
Pebble Throw 38

SCIENCE

Rock Colors 42
Where Is the Calcite? 43
Hardness Test 44
Cooking Up Igneous Rocks 45
Layers of Sediment 46
A Layered Paperweight 47
A Metamorphic Sandwich 48
Investigating Sand 49
Fossil Imprints 50
Mold and Cast Fossils 51

SOCIAL STUDIES

Rocks at Work 55
Murals of Workers 56
A Miniature Garden 57
Famous Rock Formations 58
Sandpaintings 59
What Makes a Hero? 60
A Game from Long Ago 61

ROCKS AND MINERALS CUMULATIVE TEST 62

CERTIFICATE OF COMPLETION 64

Introduction

Due to the often-changing national, state, and district standards, it is frequently difficult to "squeeze in" fascinating topics for student enrichment on top of meeting required standards and including a balanced program in your classroom curriculum. The *Stepping into Standards Theme Series* incorporates required subjects and skills for second- and third-grade students while engaging them in an exciting and meaningful theme. Students will participate in a variety of language arts experiences to help them with **reading** and **writing** skills. They will also enjoy **standards-based math activities, hands-on science projects,** and **interactive social studies activities.**

The creative lessons in *Rocks and Minerals* provide imaginative, innovative ideas to help you motivate students as they learn about rocks and minerals in your classroom. The activities will inspire students to explore rocks and minerals as well as provide them with opportunities to enhance their knowledge and meet state standards. The pretest and posttest will help you assess your students' knowledge of the subject matter and skills.

Invite students to explore rocks and minerals as they
- learn about the three groups of rocks
- discover which rocks are hard and which are soft
- improve reading comprehension while reading a mini-book about rocks
- investigate the properties of different rocks
- write descriptive poetry about rocks
- learn about famous rock formations

Each resource book in the *Stepping into Standards Theme Series* includes standards information, numerous activities, easy-to-use reproducibles, and a full-color overhead transparency to help you integrate a fun theme into your required curriculum. You will see how easy it can be to incorporate creative activities with academic requirements while students enjoy their exploration of rocks and minerals!

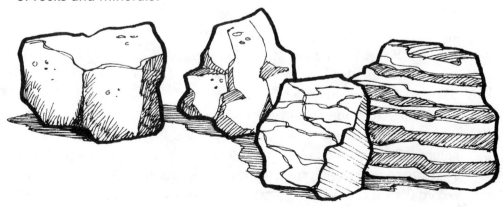

Getting Started

How to Use This Book

This comprehensive resource is filled with all the components you need to introduce, teach, review, and assess students on key skills while still making their learning experience as memorable as possible. The lessons are divided into four main sections: Language Arts, Math, Science, and Social Studies. Follow these simple steps to maximize student learning.

1 Use the **Meeting Standards** chart (pages 6–7) to help you identify the standards featured in each activity and incorporate them into your curriculum.

2 Review **Introducing . . . Rocks and Minerals** (page 8). This page provides numerous facts about the theme of study, literature selections that work well with the theme, key vocabulary words that your students will encounter while studying the theme, and the answers to all the assessments presented throughout the resource. Use this page to obtain background knowledge and ideas to help you make this a theme to remember!

3 Use the **Rocks and Minerals Pretest** (page 9) to assess your students' prior knowledge of the theme. This short, knowledge-based, multiple-choice test focuses on the key components of rocks and minerals. Use the results to help determine how much introduction to provide for the theme. The test can also be administered again at the end of the unit of study to see how much students have learned.

4 Copy the **What Do You Know? KWL Chart** (page 10) onto an overhead transparency, or enlarge it onto a piece of chart paper. Ask students to share what they already know about rocks and minerals. Record student responses in the "What We **Know**" column. Ask students to share what they would like to know about rocks and minerals. Record student responses in the "What We **Want** to Know" column. Then, set aside the chart. Revisit it at the end of the unit. Ask students to share what they learned about rocks and minerals, and record their responses in the "What We **Learned**" column.

5 Give students the **Rocks and Minerals—Reading Comprehension Test** (pages 11–12). It is a great way to introduce students to the theme while making learning interesting. You can assess your students' comprehension skills as well as introduce students to the characteristics of rocks and minerals. The multiple-choice questions require students to use literal as well as inferential skills.

6 Use the **Rocks and Minerals full-color transparency** to enhance the theme. Display the transparency at any time during the unit to support the lessons and activities and to help reinforce key concepts about rocks and minerals.

7 Use the activities from the **Language Arts, Math, Science, and Social Studies sections** (pages 13–61) to teach students about rocks and minerals and to help them learn, practice, and review the required standards for their grade level. Each activity includes a list of objectives, a materials list, and a set of easy-to-follow directions. Either complete each section in its entirety before continuing on to the next section, or mix and match activities from each section.

8 Use the skills-based **Rocks and Minerals Cumulative Test** (pages 62–63) to help you assess both what your students learned about the theme and what skills they acquired while studying the theme. It will also help you identify if students are able to apply learned skills to different situations. This cumulative test includes both multiple-choice questions and short-answer questions to provide a well-rounded assessment of your students' knowledge.

9 Upon completion of the unit, reward your students for their accomplishments with the **Certificate of Completion** (page 64). Students are sure to be eager to share their knowledge and certificate with family and friends.

Meeting Standards

Language Arts	Our Rocky Earth (PAGE 13)	Layers of the Earth (PAGE 14)	What Are Rocks? (PAGE 15)	Erupting Volcanoes (PAGE 16)	Rock Particles (PAGE 17)	Granite vs. Gneiss (PAGE 18)	Words to Know (PAGE 18)	Verb Ending Challenge (PAGE 19)	Antonym and Synonym Search (PAGE 20)	Rock Letter (PAGE 20)	Describe a Rock (PAGE 21)	If You Find a Rock (PAGE 22)	A New Ending for Sylvester (PAGE 23)	A Magic Pebble (PAGE 23)
READING														
Comprehension	●	●	●	●	●	●	●					●	●	
Literary Analysis	●			●										
Story Elements													●	●
Vocabulary Development		●	●	●	●	●	●	●			●			
Word Analysis		●					●	●						
WRITING														
Antonyms									●					
Applications										●		●		●
Friendly Letters										●				
Literary Response													●	
Main Ideas											●			
Paragraphs											●			
Revision										●			●	●
Sequencing														●
Synonyms									●					

Meeting Standards

Math
Science
Social Studies

	Weigh and Compare (PAGE 31)	Mount Rushmore—A Towering Memorial (PAGE 32)	Rocks for Sale (PAGE 33)	Shopping for Gemstones (PAGE 34)	Gemstone Geometry (PAGE 35)	Birthday Survey (PAGE 36)	How Many Pebbles? (PAGE 37)	A Game of Chance (PAGE 37)	Pebble Throw (PAGE 38)	Rock Colors (PAGE 42)	Where Is the Calcite? (PAGE 43)	Hardness Test (PAGE 44)	Cooking Up Igneous Rocks (PAGE 45)	Layers of Sediment (PAGE 46)	A Layered Paperweight (PAGE 47)	A Metamorphic Sandwich (PAGE 48)	Investigating Sand (PAGE 49)	Fossil Imprints (PAGE 50)	Mold and Cast Fossils (PAGE 51)	Rocks at Work (PAGE 55)	Murals of Workers (PAGE 56)	A Miniature Garden (PAGE 57)	Famous Rock Formations (PAGE 58)	Sandpaintings (PAGE 59)	What Makes a Hero? (PAGE 60)	A Game from Long Ago (PAGE 61)
MATH																										
Addition		•	•	•			•	•	•																	
Data Analysis & Probability	•					•	•	•	•																	
Geometry					•																					
Measurement	•	•																								
Money			•	•																						
Number & Operations		•					•		•																	
Problem Solving	•	•	•				•																			
Representation						•																				
Subtraction		•		•																						
SCIENCE																										
Investigation & Experimentation										•	•	•	•	•	•	•	•	•	•							
Properties of Earth Materials										•	•	•	•	•	•	•	•	•	•		•	•	•			
Properties of Objects & Materials										•	•	•	•	•	•	•	•	•	•	•						
SOCIAL STUDIES																										
Ancestors																									•	•
Economics																								•		
Heroes of History																					•					
Map Skills																							•			
Natural Resources																				•		•				

Introducing . . . Rocks and Minerals

FACTS ABOUT ROCKS AND MINERALS

- Rocks are made up of one or more minerals.
- A mineral is a nonliving solid found in nature.
- Rocks can be divided into three different groups based on their properties.
- Igneous rock is formed from molten rock that has cooled and hardened.
- Sedimentary rock is formed from material that has settled into layers and hardened.
- Metamorphic rock is rock that has been changed by heat and pressure.
- Fossils are the hardened remains of plants and animals.
- People use rocks in many different ways.

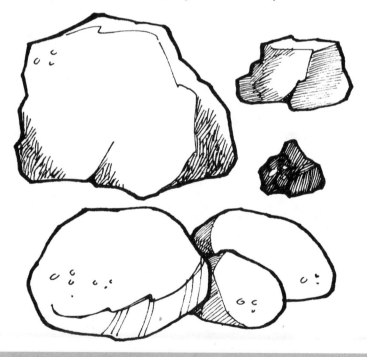

LITERATURE LINKS

A Gift from the Sea by Kate Banks (Farrar, Straus & Giroux)

If You Find a Rock by Peggy Christian (Harcourt)

The Magic School Bus Inside the Earth by Joanna Cole (Scholastic)

Return of Crazy Horse by William Kotzwinkle (Farrar, Straus & Giroux)

Rocks and Minerals by Jack Challoner (Gareth Stevens Publishing)

Rocks and Minerals: Over 100 Questions and Answers to Things You Want to Know by Anna Claybourne (Parragon)

Rushmore by Lynn Curlee (Scholastic)

Sylvester and the Magic Pebble by William Steig (Aladdin)

VOCABULARY

fossil

igneous

lava

magma

metamorphic

mineral

sediment

sedimentary

ASSESSMENT ANSWERS

Rocks and Minerals Pretest (PAGE 9)
1. *d* 2. *d* 3. *b* 4. *c* 5. *a* 6. *c* 7. *a* 8. *c*

Rocks and Minerals—Reading Comprehension Test (PAGES 11–12)
1. *c* 2. *a* 3. *b* 4. *c* 5. *d* 6. *c*

Rocks and Minerals Cumulative Test (PAGES 62–63)
1. *d* 2. *a* 3. *b* 4. *d* 5. *c* 6. *d* 7. *c* 8. *d* 9. *a* 10. *b* 11. *Answers may vary*
12. *Answers may vary*

Rocks and Minerals Pretest

Directions: Fill in the best answer for each question.

1 What are rocks made of?

ⓐ sand

ⓑ minerals

ⓒ pebbles

ⓓ all of the above

2 What is the earth's outer layer of rock called?

ⓐ core

ⓑ sediment

ⓒ mantle

ⓓ crust

3 True or False: All rocks form in layers.

ⓐ true

ⓑ false

4 Which of these is **not** a type of rock?

ⓐ granite

ⓑ limestone

ⓒ ruby

ⓓ marble

5 Why do some rocks have more than one color?

ⓐ They contain more than one mineral.

ⓑ They were scratched by other rocks.

ⓒ They were formed in the sea.

ⓓ They contain lots of sand.

6 What do we call the hardened remains of plants and animals that lived long ago?

ⓐ models

ⓑ lava

ⓒ fossils

ⓓ clay

7 True or False: Some rocks are formed from hot, molten rock.

ⓐ true

ⓑ false

8 Which statement is **not** true?

ⓐ Rocks are changed by heat and pressure.

ⓑ Rocks are useful in many ways.

ⓒ Most rocks contain only one mineral.

ⓓ Some rocks are harder than other rocks.

What Do You Know? KWL Chart

What We Know	What We Want to Know	What We Learned

Rocks and Minerals © 2003 Creative Teaching Press

Name_____ Date_____

Rocks and Minerals—
Reading Comprehension Test

Directions: Read the story and then answer the six questions.

Rocks come in many sizes, shapes, and colors. Yet all rocks are alike in one way. They are made up of minerals. A mineral is a non-living solid found in nature. Some rocks contain only one mineral. Most rocks, though, are made up of several kinds of minerals. Other rocks are made of other things, such as sand and pebbles, in addition to minerals.

When you look at rocks carefully, you will see that they have many differences. Some rocks are speckled. Others are striped. Some rocks are bumpy and rough. Others are flat and smooth. Some rocks look shiny, while others look dull.

The way a rock looks depends on the kinds of minerals it contains. It also depends on how the rock was formed. There are three main kinds of rocks: igneous, sedimentary, and metamorphic. Igneous rocks are formed from hot, molten rock that cooled and hardened. Igneous rocks that cooled quickly feel smoother than those that cooled slowly. Sedimentary rocks are formed from material that settled in layers at the bottom of oceans, lakes, and rivers. The layers were squeezed together until they changed into rock. Metamorphic rocks are igneous or sedimentary rocks that have been changed by heat and pressure. These new rocks are harder than the rocks they were made from.

Be a "rock detective." Go on a rock hunt and look closely at the rocks you find. Can you see some of the minerals? Are there any layers? How do the rocks feel? See how many different kinds of rocks you can find!

Rocks and Minerals © 2003 Creative Teaching Press

Name_____ Date_____

Rocks and Minerals—
Reading Comprehension Test

1 Which statement is **true** about all rocks?

   ⓐ All rocks are formed under the ocean.

   ⓑ All rocks come from hot, melted rock.

   ⓒ All rocks have minerals in them.

   ⓓ All rocks are bumpy and rough.

2 True or False: There are three main kinds of rocks.

   ⓐ true

   ⓑ false

3 True or False: All rocks are rough.

   ⓐ true

   ⓑ false

4 Which of these is **not** a type of rock?

   ⓐ igneous

   ⓑ metamorphic

   ⓒ mineral

   ⓓ sedimentary

5 What happens to rocks that are changed by heat and pressure?

   ⓐ They become shinier.

   ⓑ They become darker.

   ⓒ They become softer.

   ⓓ They become harder.

6 What is the main idea of the story?

   ⓐ Rocks have many colors.

   ⓑ Rocks are hard to find.

   ⓒ Rocks differ in many ways.

   ⓓ Rocks can change over time.

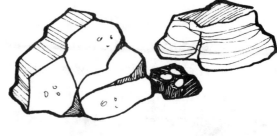

Rocks and Minerals © 2003 Creative Teaching Press

Language Arts

Our Rocky Earth

MATERIALS

- Our Rocky Earth mini-book (pages 24–26)
- Rocks and Minerals transparency
- overhead projector
- scissors
- crayons or markers

OBJECTIVE

- Students will learn the names of the three major types of rocks.

Display the Rocks and Minerals transparency. Discuss with students the different groups of rocks. Give each student the three pages of the Our Rocky Earth mini-book. Have students cut out the boxes. Then, tell them to place the pages in the correct order, starting with the title page. Staple the left side of each student's pages to create a book. Invite students to color the pictures. Explain to the class that they will be reading their book on numerous days. They will also be using their book for additional activities. Ask students to look through their book and determine the three types of rocks they will be learning about. Lead students to say *igneous, sedimentary,* and *metamorphic.* Record the three types of rocks on the board. Point out the different types of rocks to students. Pronounce the name of each type of rock and discuss its characteristics. Explain to students that they will learn more about each type of rock when they read their mini-book. Either collect the mini-books and redistribute them when needed, or have students keep their book in their desk.

MATERIALS

- globe
- apple
- knife (adult use only)
- completed Our Rocky Earth mini-books (see page 13)

OBJECTIVES

Students will
- learn about the layers of the earth.
- answer questions about the layers of the earth.

Show the class a globe and an apple. Ask students to share what they know about a globe. Lead students to share that a globe is a replica of Earth. Hold up the apple. Explain to the class that like an apple, Earth has many layers. Carefully slice the apple in half, and show one half to the class. Point out the different layers of the apple (i.e., skin, flesh, core). Point to the apple's skin. Tell students that the outer layer of the earth is called the crust. It is much thinner than the other layers, just like the skin of an apple. Point to the apple's flesh. Tell students this part of the earth is called the mantle. Explain that the layer under the crust (the mantle) is the thickest layer. Point to the apple's center. Explain that the center of the earth is the innermost layer. Like an apple, it is called the core. As a class, have students read aloud page 1 in their Our Rocky Earth mini-book. Then, ask them the following questions:

- *What are the three layers of the earth?* (crust, mantle, core)
- *Why can't you see all of the earth's crust?* (Some parts of the crust lie under the ocean.)
- *Why do scientists know so little about the mantle and core?* (They cannot go deep into the earth and see the layers.)

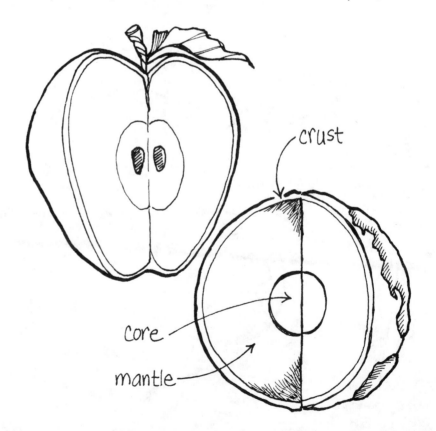

What Are Rocks?

OBJECTIVES

Students will
- identify various characteristics of rocks.
- answer questions about rocks.

MATERIALS

- assortment of rocks
- magnifying glasses
- completed Our Rocky Earth mini-books (see page 13)

Display a variety of rocks for students to examine. Encourage students to use a magnifying glass to examine the rocks more closely. Have students point out the differences they see in color, shape, and texture. Record student responses on the board. Divide the class into pairs. Have partners read page 2 in their Our Rocky Earth mini-book. Then, invite the class to discuss the following questions:

- *What do all rocks have in common?* (They are made of minerals. They are nonliving.)

- *Do most rocks contain only one mineral or more than one?* (Most rocks contain more than one mineral.)

- *Why is it sometimes hard to see the different kinds of minerals in a rock?* (The minerals have the same colors. The minerals are very small.)

Erupting Volcanoes

- picture of a volcano erupting
- balloon
- water
- pin
- completed Our Rocky Earth mini-books (see page 13)
- samples and/or pictures of igneous rocks, such as granite, basalt, and obsidian (optional)
- magnifying glasses (optional)

OBJECTIVES

Students will
- understand how lava escapes from volcanoes.
- read information to learn what role magma plays in the formation of rocks.

Show the class a picture of a volcano erupting. Point out the lava coming from the volcano. Explain that the lava comes from hot, melted rock that is deep inside the earth. This melted rock, called magma, is under great pressure. Present this simple demonstration to show what happens to magma. Fill a balloon with water. Tie a knot at the end of the balloon. Tell the class to imagine that the water is magma. Squeeze the balloon gently. Ask students to share what they notice. Students will observe that the water moves. Explain that magma gets squeezed from place to place deep inside the earth. Next, hold the balloon over a sink or take it outdoors. Have the class observe what happens when, while squeezing the balloon, you puncture it with a pin. (The water shoots out.) Explain that like the water that shot out of the hole in the balloon, magma sometimes shoots out through an opening in the earth's surface. As a class, read page 3 in the Our Rocky Earth mini-book to find out what role magma plays in the formation of rocks. Tell students that when magma cools, it changes to solid rock. To extend the activity, display pictures and samples of igneous rocks. Encourage students to use magnifying glasses to observe the characteristics of igneous rocks.

Rock Particles

MATERIALS

● completed Our Rocky Earth mini-books (see page 13)

● samples and pictures of sedimentary rocks (such as sandstone, limestone, coal, and shale)

● magnifying glasses

● drawing paper

● crayons or markers

OBJECTIVES

Students will
● observe sedimentary rocks.
● learn about the different sediments found in sedimentary rocks.
● write a narrative story that describes the journey of a rock.

Tell the class that they are going to be "rock detectives." Take the class to the playground, and have students look for sedimentary rocks and small soil particles. Return to the classroom, and discuss with students where they found the particles and where the particles might have come from. Explain that the particles were probably moved to the schoolyard by wind and rain. Tell the class that sometimes tiny rock particles, like the ones in the schoolyard, are washed into lakes, rivers, and oceans. These particles, called sediments, drop to the bottom and settle into layers. Have students read page 4 in their Our Rocky Earth mini-book to find out about different sediments and the rocks they form. Then, display samples and pictures of sedimentary rocks for students to examine. Encourage students to use magnifying glasses to observe details of rocks. Give each student a piece of drawing paper. Have students draw and label the layers of a sedimentary rock. Then, have them write about where they think the rock came from. Encourage students to pretend to be the rock and describe the journey it traveled to get to its current location. Invite volunteers to share their completed paper with the class.

Granite vs. Gneiss

OBJECTIVE

- Students will distinguish between granite and gneiss.

Show the class samples or pictures of granite and gneiss ('nīs). Ask students to describe how the rocks are different. (Granite is speckled; gneiss is striped.) Record student responses on the board. Tell the class that one of the rocks was formed from the other. Have students guess which one changed. Then, hold up the granite. Explain that granite, under great heat and pressure, changes into a new rock called gneiss. Have students read page 5 in their Our Rocky Earth mini-book to find out about other rocks that change. Students should learn that shale changes to slate and limestone changes to marble. Then, display the samples or pictures of metamorphic rocks. Have students discuss any changes they see in the rocks.

Words to Know

OBJECTIVE

- Students will match rock vocabulary words with the correct definitions.

Display the Rocks and Minerals transparency. Review with students the characteristics of sedimentary, metamorphic, and igneous rocks. Give each student a Words to Know reproducible. Invite volunteers to read aloud the words in the word bank. Have students match each word with its definition. Check the answers together. (Students should write 1. *b* 2. *e* 3. *d* 4. *g* 5. *i* 6. *h* 7. *f* 8. *c* 9. *a* 10. *k* 11. *j*.) List on a chart the vocabulary words and the names of rocks the class has learned. Display the chart for student reference. As students continue their rock study, have them add other words to the list.

Verb Ending Challenge

MATERIALS

● completed Our Rocky Earth mini-books (see page 13)

OBJECTIVE

● Students will add *-ed* and *-ing* endings to verbs.

Review with the class the rules for adding *-ed* and *-ing* to the end of verbs. Write verbs such as *walk, hike, stop,* and *hurry* on the board. Discuss what kinds of words need to be changed when *-ed* and *-ing* are added. (Example: Words with a silent *e* at the end must drop the *e* before adding the ending.) Ask students to come up to the board and add the verb endings *-ed* and *-ing* to the words. Next, write on the board verbs from the Our Rocky Earth mini-book (e.g., *melt, appear, change, squeeze, believe, trap, bury, carry*). Have students copy the words on a piece of paper. Then, have them add *-ed* and *-ing* to each word. Invite volunteers to share their answers with the class. To extend the activity, have students find other verbs from their mini-book to add to their list. Then, ask students to add *-ed* and *-ing* to these words.

MATERIALS

- Antonym and Synonym Search reproducible (page 28)
- completed Our Rocky Earth mini-books (see page 13)

Antonym and Synonym Search

OBJECTIVE

- Students will demonstrate their understanding of antonyms and synonyms.

Review with students that antonyms are words that mean the opposite and synonyms are words that mean the same. Divide the class into pairs. Give each pair of students an Antonym and Synonym Search reproducible. Tell students they will pretend to be detectives and search through their Our Rocky Earth mini-book to find the antonyms and synonyms listed on their reproducible. Once students have completed their search, review the answers as a class.

Name Jack and Jane   Date March 10, 2004

Antonym and Synonym Search

Page 1
antonym of **inner** outer   synonym of **under** below
antonym of **freeze** melt   synonym of **big** huge

Page 2
antonym of **smooth** rough   synonym of **circular** round
antonym of **same** different   synonym of **tough** hard

Page 3
antonym of **quickly** slowly   synonym of **melted** molten
antonym of **cold** hot   synonym of **force** pressure

Page 4
antonym of **small** large   synonym of **small** tiny
antonym of **up** down   synonym of **made** formed

Page 5
antonym of **soft** hard   synonym of **stripes** bands
antonym of **old** new   synonym of **spotted** speckled

MATERIALS

- *Rocks and Minerals: Over 100 Questions and Answers to Things You Want to Know* by Anna Claybourne

Rock Letter

OBJECTIVE

- Students will write a friendly letter.

Read numerous pages of *Rocks and Minerals* to the class. Discuss with students different facts they learned from the book. Review how to write a friendly letter. Discuss the salutation, greeting, body, closing, and signature. Tell students that they are going to write a friendly letter to a family member describing what they have learned about rocks so far. Have students include at least four interesting facts about rocks in their letter. Invite volunteers to share their letter with the class.

Describe a Rock

MATERIALS

- My Special Rock reproducible (page 29)
- chart paper
- large rock with interesting features
- rock samples

OBJECTIVE

● Students will write a series of paragraphs to describe a rock.

Copy the three sections of the My Special Rock reproducible onto three pieces of chart paper. Hold up a large rock for students to examine. Tell students to describe what they see. Next, display the prepared charts. Tell students that they are going to use the charts to help organize their observations. Have the class brainstorm words and phrases that describe the rock's shape and texture, color and design (e.g., stripes, speckles), and luster. Write each response on the corresponding chart. Have the class help you write a three-paragraph description of the rock—one paragraph for each of the three charts. Begin by directing students to the first chart, and have the class suggest a topic sentence for a paragraph describing the rock's shape and texture (e.g., *Our rock has an interesting shape and texture*). Write the suggested sentence on the board. Have students continue by dictating to you additional sentences that support the topic sentence. Write these sentences on the board to complete the first paragraph. Repeat the procedure for the other two paragraphs. Read the completed paragraphs together. Discuss how the charts helped students organize the information so that the sentences in each paragraph related to one another. Give each student a My Special Rock reproducible and a rock sample. Have students complete the reproducible about their rock and then write a three-paragraph description about it.

- *If You Find a Rock* by Peggy Christian
- crayons or markers

If You Find a Rock

OBJECTIVE

● Students will write a paragraph about a rock.

Read aloud *If You Find a Rock.* As you read the book, share the warm, thought-provoking photographs that accompany each description. Then, discuss with the class the various kinds of rocks featured in the book. Record the names of the rocks on the board. Then, have students think of other types of rocks that the author might have included. Add their ideas to the list. The following are some examples:

● a collecting rock (a rock that would be fun to collect)

● a giving rock (a rock that would make a good gift)

● crunching rocks (rocks that make pleasant crunching sounds when stepped on)

● tapping rocks (a pair of rocks that make "music" when tapped together)

Read aloud the paragraph shown below. Explain that this is an example of a paragraph about tapping rocks. Invite students to select a rock from the board. Have them write a paragraph that teaches the reader something about their chosen rock. Have students write three to five sentences. Then, invite them to illustrate their paragraph. Divide the class into pairs. Invite partners to read each other's paragraph and provide feedback about it. Have students use their partner's suggestions to revise their paragraph and then write a final draft. Compile the paragraphs in a class book titled *If You Find a Rock.*

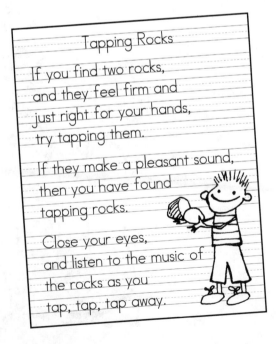

Tapping Rocks

If you find two rocks,
and they feel firm and
just right for your hands,
try tapping them.

If they make a pleasant sound,
then you have found
tapping rocks.

Close your eyes,
and listen to the music of
the rocks as you
tap, tap, tap away.

A New Ending for Sylvester

OBJECTIVE

● Students will write a new ending for a story.

Read *Sylvester and the Magic Pebble* to the class. Discuss with the class the main events in the story. Ask students *How do you think Sylvester felt when he first discovered that the pebble was magic?* (excited, amazed, overjoyed) *Why did he do such a foolish thing as to wish he were a rock?* (He panicked.) *How do you think he felt when he saw that he was a rock?* (shocked, frantic) Next, have students imagine how different the story would have been if the lion had not appeared and Sylvester had not wished he were a rock. Discuss what might have happened instead. (For example, Sylvester might have taken the pebble home right away to show his parents.) Have students work in small groups and brainstorm alternative endings to the story. Then, have the groups write their own version of the book. Encourage students to write at least a one-page story. Invite groups to read their version of the story to the class and explain why they made the changes they did.

A Magic Pebble

OBJECTIVES

Students will
● write a story with a logical sequence of events.
● write a final draft.

Read aloud *Sylvester and the Magic Pebble.* Discuss with the class what made the pebble in the story magical. Give each student a pebble. Have students close their eyes as they feel the pebble in their hands. Tell them to imagine that their pebble is a magic pebble like Sylvester's and that it can grant three wishes. Have students continue to keep their eyes closed and imagine what they would wish for. Next, give each student an If I Had a Magic Pebble reproducible. Have students answer the questions on their reproducible to help them plan a story about their magic pebble. Then, review with students how to use their information to write a story that follows a logical sequence of events. Have students write a draft on the bottom of their reproducible and then write a revised story on a separate piece of paper. Invite volunteers to share their story with the class.

Our Rocky Earth

_____
(Name)

The earth is made up of mostly rock. In fact, you could call it one huge rock! If you could cut the earth open, you would see three layers.

The outer layer is the **crust**. It is a rocky "skin" that covers the whole earth. Parts of the crust can be seen as land. Other parts cannot be seen because they lie under the ocean.

Below the crust is the **mantle**. It is the thickest layer of the earth. It is so hot in the mantle that the rock there is soft.

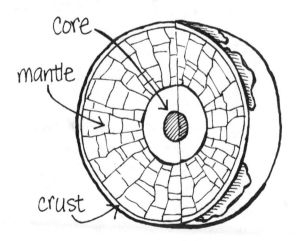

At the center of the earth is the **core.** It has two parts. The outer core is thought to be a shell of melted metal. The inner core is thought to be a solid ball of metal. Even though it is very hot in the inner core, the pressure there is so great that the core cannot melt.

1

Our Rocky Earth

What Are Rocks?

Rocks come in many different colors, shapes, and textures. Some rocks are dark-colored. Others are light-colored. Some rocks are flat. Others are round. Some rocks feel rough. Others feel smooth. All the rocks in the world, though, are alike in one way. They are made up of minerals. A **mineral** is a nonliving solid found in nature. "Nonliving" means that it was never part of a living thing, such as a plant or an animal.

Some rocks are made up of only one mineral. However, most rocks contain more than one mineral. When the minerals have different colors, they are easy to see in a rock. Sometimes, the minerals in a rock have the same colors. Then it may be hard to tell them apart just by looking at the rock. Sometimes, the minerals are very tiny and hard to see. Scientists have ways to test rocks to see what minerals are in them.

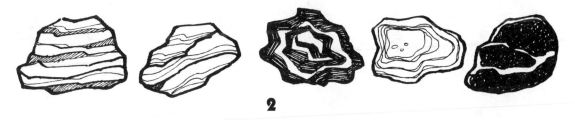

2

Igneous Rocks

It is so hot deep inside the earth that the rock there is molten, or melted. This molten rock is called **magma**.

Magma is under great pressure. Sometimes it rises to the surface of the earth through cracks in the crust. When it cools, it changes to solid rock. Rocks that are formed from magma are called **igneous rocks**.

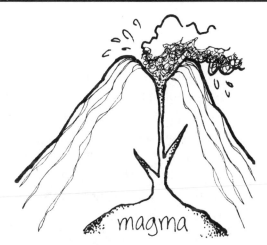

A **volcano** is a hill or mountain created by the buildup of lava or rock fragments around the opening of the earth's surface. The opening of a volcano is called a **vent**. Once magma has reached the surface, it is called **lava**. Lava cools and hardens quickly. Obsidian is an igneous rock formed in this way.

Sometimes magma gets trapped in cracks below the earth's surface. When this happens, magma cools slowly under the ground. Granite is an igneous rock formed in this way.

3

Our Rocky Earth

Sedimentary Rocks

Large rocks can be broken down into smaller rocks by wind and water. These small rocks can break down into very tiny pieces. The pieces are carried away by rain into lakes, rivers, and oceans. The tiny pieces are called **sediments.** Slowly, the sediments build up in layers. The layers become buried and pressed down. After a long time, the sediments harden and become **sedimentary rocks.**

Different sedimentary rocks come from different kinds of sediments. For example, sandstone is formed from grains of sand. Sometimes, the remains of tiny plants or animals become part of sediments. Coal is formed from the remains of plants that lived long ago. Chalk is formed from the bones of tiny sea animals.

Coal
Chalk
Sandstone

4

Metamorphic Rocks

Sometimes igneous and sedimentary rocks that are buried deep in the earth can be changed by heat and pressure. When this happens, they become a new kind of rock. These new rocks are called **metamorphic rocks.** The word *metamorphic* means "changed."

Metamorphic rocks look different from the rocks they were formed from. For example, granite is an igneous rock that is speckled. When granite changes, it becomes gneiss. The minerals in gneiss appear as bands of color. Shale, a soft sedimentary rock, hardens into slate. Limestone, another sedimentary rock, changes into marble. Marble is a very hard rock. It is used for making buildings and sculptures.

Slate
Marble
Gneiss

5

Name_____ Date_____

Words to Know

Directions: Write the letter of the word that matches each definition.

1 the outer layer of the earth _____

2 hot, melted rock _____

3 magma that has reached the earth's surface _____

4 rocks changed by heat and pressure _____

5 tiny pieces of rock material carried by water _____

6 a nonliving solid found in nature _____

7 the thick layer of rock under the crust _____

8 rocks formed from magma _____

9 the inner layer that forms the center of the earth _____

10 an opening through which magma escapes to the earth's surface _____

11 rocks formed from sediments that have hardened _____

a. core	g. metamorphic rocks
b. crust	h. mineral
c. igneous rocks	i. sediments
d. lava	j. sedimentary rocks
e. magma	k. volcano
f. mantle	

Antonym and Synonym Search

Page 1

antonym of **inner** _____   synonym of **under** _____

antonym of **freeze** _____   synonym of **big**_____

· ·

Page 2

antonym of **smooth** _____   synonym of **circular**_____

antonym of **same**_____   synonym of **tough** _____

· ·

Page 3

antonym of **quickly** _____   synonym of **melted** _____

antonym of **cold** _____   synonym of **force**_____

· ·

Page 4

antonym of **small**_____   synonym of **small**_____

antonym of **up**_____   synonym of **made** _____

· ·

Page 5

antonym of **soft** _____   synonym of **stripes** _____

antonym of **old** _____   synonym of **spotted** _____

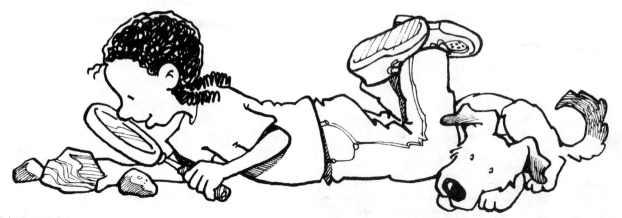

Rocks and Minerals © 2003 Creative Teaching Press

Name_____ Date_____

My Special Rock

Directions: Study your rock carefully. Answer the following questions.

Shape and Texture

The shape of the rock is

- ☐ rough
- ☐ smooth
- ☐ bumpy
- ☐ flat
- ☐ sharp
- ☐ round

Color and Design

The rock has

- ☐ speckles
- ☐ stripes

What colors do you see in the rock? _____

_____

What do the minerals that make up the rock look like? Are all of them the same size?

_____

_____

Luster (how an object shines)

The rock is

- ☐ dull
- ☐ shiny

Do some parts seem more shiny than others? _____ If so, which parts?

_____

If the rock is shiny, does it look pearly (like a pearl) or glassy (like a piece of glass)?

_____

Name_____   Date_____

If I Had a Magic Pebble

Directions: Imagine that you found a pebble that could grant three wishes. Write a story about what happened. Here are some questions your story should answer.

1 Where did you find your pebble?

2 What did it look like?

3 What did you do with it?

4 Who did you tell about your pebble?

5 Describe your three wishes.

On the pebble below, write four things that will happen in your story.

Write your final story on a separate piece of paper.

Rocks and Minerals © 2003 Creative Teaching Press

Math

Weigh and Compare

OBJECTIVES

Students will
- predict the weight of five rocks.
- use a balance scale to weigh rocks.
- compare predictions with actual weights of rocks.

Divide the class into small groups. Give each group five rocks, masking tape, a marker, a piece of scrap paper, gram cubes, and a balance scale. Tell group members to use the masking tape and marker to label their rocks *A, B, C, D,* and *E.* Have each group member hold one rock at a time and estimate which rocks are lighter and which ones are heavier. Tell group members to arrange the rocks in a line, from the lightest to the heaviest. Have students record their estimation on their paper. Have groups weigh each rock on their balance scale. Show group members how to place one of their rocks on one side of the balance scale and add gram cubes to the other side until both sides are even. Have students count the number of gram cubes used to balance the scale and record the number next to the corresponding rock on their paper. Invite groups to repeat this process with the remaining rocks. Then, based on the measurements, have groups arrange the rocks in order from the lightest to the heaviest and record the letters of the rocks on their paper. Discuss with groups their findings and how accurate their estimate was.

- assortment of small rocks
- masking tape
- marker
- scrap paper
- gram cubes
- balance scales

- *Rushmore* by Lynn Curlee
- Mount Rushmore Math reproducible (page 39)
- picture of Mount Rushmore

Mount Rushmore— A Towering Memorial

OBJECTIVE

- Students will use various operations to solve math problems.

Hold up for the class a picture of Mount Rushmore. Explain that it is a memorial to four great American presidents. Ask students to identify the four figures (George Washington, Thomas Jefferson, Theodore Roosevelt, Abraham Lincoln). Tell the class that the figures are carved on a granite cliff in the Black Hills of South Dakota. Inform students that the carving is so huge that each head is as high as five classrooms stacked on top of one another! Read *Rushmore* with the class. Discuss with students how the Mount Rushmore National Memorial was conceived, designed, and created. Then, give each student a Mount Rushmore Math reproducible. Have students work with a partner or in a small group to read and solve the problems on the reproducible in order to learn more interesting facts about one of America's most famous memorials. Students should answer 1. *14 years* 2. *answers will vary depending on the current year* 3. *60 years* 4. *24 feet (7.2 m)* 5. *240 feet (73.2 m)* 6. *60 inches (1.5 m)* 7. *$10.00.*

Rocks for Sale

OBJECTIVES

Students will
- pretend to purchase rocks.
- determine the correct amount of money needed to pay for chosen items.

MATERIALS

- assortment of rocks and pebbles
- egg cartons or resealable plastic bags
- paper strips
- play money
- scratch paper

Collect a variety of rocks for a classroom "store." Have students contribute interesting rocks that they find while outside of the classroom. Set up the store in a corner of the classroom. Display the rocks in egg cartons or resealable plastic bags. Write prices ranging from 50 cents to $2.00 on separate paper strips. Attach a price tag to each rock. Next, give each student an equal amount of toy coins and bills. Let a small group of students at a time visit the store. Have each student point to two or more rocks he or she would like to buy. Have students calculate their costs on scratch paper and show you the amount they owe. If a student's total is correct and he or she can accurately choose the money needed to pay for the rocks, then allow the student to take the selected rocks and keep them as souvenirs of the rock study. If the total is incorrect, have the student recalculate the total cost. If the student is still having a difficult time, ask him or her to work with a partner to solve the problem. To extend the activity, have students determine the type of rocks they purchased from the classroom store.

- Buy Me a Gemstone reproducible (page 40)

- catalogs or store flyers that feature jewelry

Shopping for Gemstones

OBJECTIVE

- Students will determine differences in cost among various items.

Ask students to recall what rocks are made of (nonliving materials that occur in nature called minerals). Tell students that some minerals are prized for their great beauty. These minerals are called *gemstones,* and they are often used to make jewelry. Show the class pictures of jewelry made from gemstones, such as a diamond ring or a ruby necklace. Ask students to name some reasons why a person might buy jewelry (e.g., to give a gift, to mark an occasion such as an engagement or anniversary, to have an eye-catching accessory). Divide the class into small groups. Give each student a Buy Me a Gemstone reproducible, and give each group catalogs or store flyers that feature jewelry. Have students pretend that they are shopping for jewelry that contains one or more gemstones. Have each group member select one page from a catalog or store flyer to use to answer the questions on the reproducible. Have students share their results with their group.

DiBeen's Jewelry Store

$250.00

$160.00

$2,900.00

FINE JEWELRY

Gemstone Geometry

MATERIALS

OBJECTIVE

- Students will recognize and sort geometric shapes.

- pictures of natural and cut gemstones
- catalogs and store flyers that feature jewelry
- scissors
- chart paper
- glue

Display pictures of jewelry that contains gemstones. Point out to the class that the gemstones are polished and have geometric shapes. Also, show students pictures of "natural, uncut" gemstones. Point out the characteristics of the natural gemstones. Students should see that gemstones in nature have a rough surface and an irregular shape. Explain that skilled gem cutters cut and polish the stones in order to make them beautiful and more valuable. Give each pair of students a catalog and flyer that feature jewelry. Have partners cut out pictures of gemstones and sort them according to their shapes. Divide a piece of chart paper into six sections. Label each section with the name of a geometric shape, such as square, oval, hexagon, circle, rectangle, and rhombus. Invite partners to glue their pictures in the appropriate sections of the chart. When finished, explain to the class that the completed chart represents the wide variety of shapes gemstones can be cut into.

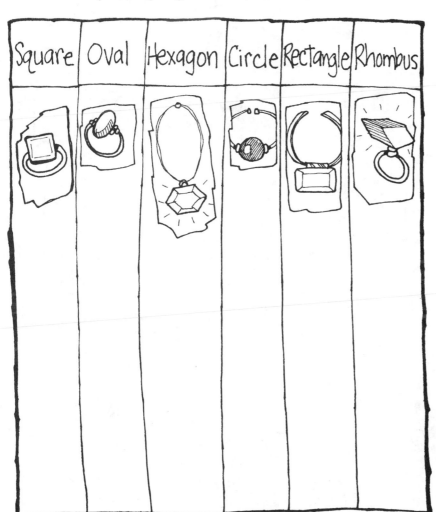

Birthday Survey

OBJECTIVES

Students will
● make a picture graph using information from a survey.
● use the results of the picture graph to help them answer questions.

Show the class pictures of birthstones, such as a diamond, emerald, sapphire, and ruby. Ask students if they know what these gemstones have in common. (They are all birthstones.) Explain that a birthstone is a gem associated with a month of the year. Many people wear rings and other jewelry made with their birthstone. According to tradition, a person's birthstone is supposed to bring good luck. Write on the board the months of the year in a column. Ask each student to share his or her birthday with the class. Write each student's name in the correct row. Give each student a Birthday Survey. Have students use the information from the board to make a picture graph on their reproducible to display the results. Have students answer the questions at the bottom of their reproducible. Invite volunteers to share their answers with the class.

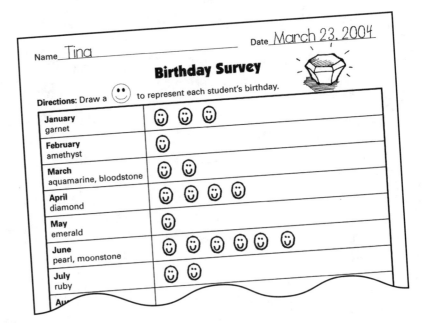

How Many Pebbles?

- glass jar with lid
- pebbles (or small rocks)
- slips of paper

OBJECTIVE

- Students will develop a strategy for estimating the number of items in a jar.

Fill a jar with pebbles, and tighten the lid. Give each student a slip of paper. Have students think of a strategy to best estimate the number of pebbles in the jar. Have students write their estimate on their paper. Have them share their estimation and what strategy they used to arrive at their answer. Determine how many students used the same strategy and how many different strategies they used. Discuss the results with the class. Then, let the class help you count the pebbles to determine who had the closest estimate.

A Game of Chance

MATERIALS

- 2 dark-colored rocks for each pair
- 2 light-colored rocks for each pair
- paper bags
- drawing paper

OBJECTIVE

- Students will describe events as likely or unlikely and test their predictions.

Divide the class into pairs. Give each pair two dark-colored rocks, two light-colored rocks, a paper bag, and a piece of drawing paper. Have students draw two columns on their paper and label them *Dark* and *Light.* Tell students to place their rocks in the bag. Ask *Is there a better chance of drawing a dark-colored rock or a light-colored rock?* Have students write their prediction on their paper. Have students take turns shaking the bag and drawing a rock without looking. After they draw each rock, have partners make a tally mark to show what color of rock they chose. Have students return the rock to the bag and continue drawing rocks until they have recorded ten tally marks. When students are finished, discuss with the class the results and their predictions. Students should determine that they were just as likely to draw a dark-colored rock as they were to draw a light-colored rock. Then, have students set aside one of the light-colored rocks. Have them predict what would happen if they played again and then test their predictions. Discuss the results. Students should determine they were more likely to draw a dark-colored rock than a light-colored one. Ask students how they could change the game so that there would be a greater chance of drawing a light-colored rock. Have students test their predictions.

Pebble Throw

OBJECTIVES

Students will
● add numbers to reach a desired total.
● collect data.

In advance, collect five pebbles for each pair of students. Dab some paint on one side of each pebble. Let the paint dry completely before giving the pebbles to students. Divide the class into partners. Assign each pair of students a place to sit down on a carpeted area, or place a piece of felt in front of them to keep the noise level to a minimum. Give each pair five pebbles and a piece of paper. Tell partners they will take turns throwing the pebbles in the air and counting the number of pebbles that land with the paint side up. Explain that the player who gets to 50 first wins the game. Have partners count how many pebbles land with their painted side up each time and record that number on their paper. Ask partners to total their points after each round. To extend the activity, have players record the number of pebbles that land with the painted side up and the number that land with the painted side down each time. After ten throws, have partners tally how many pebbles there were of each. Explain that the player whose total number of pebbles with the painted side up was greater than the total number of pebbles with the painted side down is the winner.

Mount Rushmore Math

Mount Rushmore is a huge carving of four presidents. The four faces are carved on a granite cliff in the Black Hills of South Dakota. The carving was designed by a sculptor named Gutzon Borglum.

Directions: Solve the following problems.

1 The work on Mount Rushmore began in 1927 and ended in 1941. How many years did the project take?

2 How long ago has it been since Mount Rushmore was completed?

3 Gutzon Borglum was born in 1867. How old was he when he began working on Mount Rushmore?

4 The head of each president is 60 feet (18.3 meters) high—as high as a five-story building! If 60 feet (18.3 meters) equals 5 stories, how many feet equals 2 stories?

5 Suppose all four heads were stacked on top of one another to form a tower. How high would the tower be?

6 Borglum made a small model of his sculpture. One inch (2.5 centimeters) on the model stood for 12 inches (30.5 centimeters) on the mountain. How tall was the model for each president's head?

7 Gutzon Borglum hired 400 men to work on Mount Rushmore. A worker earned $1.25 an hour. How much money did a worker earn in 8 hours?

Name_____ Date_____

Buy Me a Gemstone

Directions: Use the information on your catalog page to answer the following questions.

How much is the most expensive item on the page? _____

What kind of gemstone is used in the jewelry?_____

How much is the least expensive item on the page? _____

What kind of gemstone is used in the jewelry?_____

What is the difference in cost between the most expensive item and the

least expensive item? _____

How many items on the page cost more than $50.00? _____

How many items cost less than $50.00? _____

Choose two items. How much would they cost to buy?

_____

Suppose you had $100.00 to spend. Could you buy any of the items on the page?

_____

If so, which item would you buy?

_____

How much change would you get back?_____

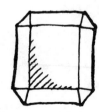

Name_____ Date_____

Birthday Survey

Directions: Draw a 😊 to represent each student's birthday.

January garnet	
February amethyst	
March aquamarine, bloodstone	
April diamond	
May emerald	
June pearl, moonstone	
July ruby	
August peridot, sardonyx	
September sapphire	
October opal, tourmaline	
November topaz	
December turquoise, zircon	

😊 = 1 student

Which month had the greatest number of birthdays? _____

Which month had the least number of birthdays? _____

How many students have diamond as their birthstone? _____

Which is greater—the number of students who have garnet as their birthstone

or the number of students who have amethyst? _____

MATERIALS

- Rock Colors reproducible (page 52)
- assortment of rocks in different colors
- resealable plastic bags
- pictures of rocks (optional)
- magnifying glasses

Rock Colors

OBJECTIVE

- Students will examine and compare the colors in rock samples.

In advance, place five rocks in a resealable bag for each pair of students. Show the class two different rocks or pictures of rocks. Ask students to name the colors they see. Display other rocks, and encourage students to notice that rocks come in a variety of colors. Tell the class that the different colors in a rock indicate the different minerals that make up the rock. Give each student a Rock Colors reproducible and a magnifying glass. Divide the class into pairs. Give each pair of students a bag of rocks. Tell students to check off the colors that their rocks contain and answer the questions at the bottom of their reproducible. Then, discuss with the class the fact that most rocks contain various colors. Lead students to conclude from looking at their rock samples that most rocks are made up of a combination of minerals. Invite students to share their answers with the class. (Note: The different minerals in a rock can often be distinguished by their different colors. However, if mineral grains are tiny and the colors are similar, then it is not always possible to tell the different minerals apart just by looking at the rock.)

Where Is the Calcite?

MATERIALS

- seashells
- pieces of limestone, chalk, and other assorted rocks
- plastic spoons
- small plastic plates
- paper towels
- clear, plastic cups
- vinegar

OBJECTIVE

- Students will test rocks for the presence of calcite.

Divide the class into small groups. Give each group a seashell, a piece of limestone, a piece of chalk, two or three different rocks, a plastic spoon, a small plastic plate, a paper towel, and a plastic cup half-filled with vinegar. Ask group members to predict what will happen when they place the various items into the cup of vinegar. Record student responses on the board. Have group members place their shell in the cup of vinegar and observe what happens. (Bubbles begin to rise from the shell.) Tell the class that the vinegar is an acid and that the shell contains the mineral calcite. Explain that the calcite reacts with the acid to produce carbon dioxide, a gas. This causes the bubbling. Have students use the spoon to carefully take the shell out of the cup and place it on the paper towel to dry. Next, tell the class that some rocks contain calcite. Have students repeat the "vinegar test" on their chalk, their limestone, and their other rocks to see if they contain calcite. Point out that chalk occurs in nature as a soft, white rock. The chalk used for chalkboards is made from natural chalk. Discuss the results with the class. Students will discover that the limestone and chalk react with the vinegar, forming bubbles like the shell did. Lead students to conclude that limestone and chalk both contain calcite. (Note: Replenish the vinegar as needed if you notice it is losing its effectiveness after several items are placed in it.)

Hardness Test

MATERIALS

- Hardness Test reproducible (page 53)
- Rocks and Minerals transparency
- masking tape
- soft, medium, and hard rocks
- resealable plastic bags
- nails
- wet paper towels
- overhead projector

OBJECTIVE

- Students will compare the hardness of rocks using scratch tests.

In advance, use masking tape to label three rocks from 1 to 3 for each pair of students. Place each set of rocks in a resealable plastic bag. Explain to the class that they are going to test an assortment of rocks to determine which rocks are harder than others. Tell students that scientists test the hardness of rocks in order to categorize them. Have students work in pairs. Give each pair a nail, a wet paper towel, a bag of rocks, and a Hardness Test reproducible. Tell students to first try scratching each rock with their fingernail and record their results on their reproducible. Then, have students try scratching each rock with the nail and record their results. To check that they actually made a scratch, tell students to wipe the rock each time with a damp paper towel. Explain that a scratch exists if the mark remains on the rock after the rock has dried. Tell students that a rock that can be scratched by a fingernail is very soft. A rock that can be scratched by a nail, but not by a fingernail, is much harder. Display the Rocks and Minerals transparency. Point to different rocks, and ask students to determine if the rock would be hard or soft.

Cooking Up Igneous Rocks

- small mixing bowl
- medium-sized bowl
- ice cubes
- electric frying pan
- ½ cup water
- 2½ cups sugar
- wooden spoon
- ladle
- assorted igneous rocks (optional)

OBJECTIVE

- Students will observe how the rate of an igneous rock's cooling affects the size of its crystals.

At least 1 hour before the lesson, place a small mixing bowl in the refrigerator to chill. When you are ready to start the activity, place the chilled bowl in a medium-sized bowl half-filled with ice cubes in order to keep it chilled. Explain to the class that you will use an electric frying pan to make a batch of "igneous rocks." (Let students stand close enough to watch, but do not let them get too close to the pan.) Bring the water to a boil in the pan. Gradually add the sugar. Over medium heat, stir the mixture continually with a wooden spoon to dissolve the sugar. Be careful that the sugar does not burn. When all of the sugar is dissolved, turn off the heat. Use a ladle to spoon half of the mixture into the chilled bowl. Leave the rest of the mixture in the pan to cool slowly. After a few minutes, let the class compare the two mixtures. Students should discover that the mixture in the bowl has tiny grains and is smooth. The mixture in the pan is coarse and lumpy. Explain that because the mixture in the chilled bowl cooled quickly, only tiny crystals (grains) were produced. The mixture in the pan, however, cooled more slowly, allowing larger crystals to form. Tell the class that igneous rocks are formed by molten rock called magma. When magma cools, it hardens. The minerals in rocks usually form crystals that lock together. Igneous rocks that have cooled quickly have small crystals and a smooth texture. These rocks are fine-grained. Igneous rocks that have cooled slowly have large crystals and a rough texture. Rocks with large crystals are coarse-grained. To extend the activity, have the class examine igneous rocks, such as granite and basalt. Ask students to guess which rocks cooled quickly and which cooled slowly. For example, the granite is coarse-grained and rough; it cooled slowly. The basalt is fine-grained and smooth; it cooled quickly.

Layers of Sediment

- Layers of Sediment reproducible (page 54)
- sand
- gravel
- soil
- 3 plastic bins
- plastic cups
- large, clear jar with lid (e.g., mayonnaise jars) for each pair
- water

OBJECTIVE

- Students will observe how sedimentary rocks form in layers.

Place sand, gravel, and soil in separate plastic bins. Place a plastic cup in each bin. Divide the class into pairs. Give each pair a Layers of Sediment reproducible and a jar. Have a few pairs of students at a time pour ½ cup each of gravel, sand, and soil into their jar in any order. Then, have students fill their jar three-fourths full with water and screw on the lid. Ask students to predict what will happen when they shake their jar. Tell them to record their prediction on their reproducible. Have partners shake their jar up and down several times. Ask students to predict what will happen to the materials inside the jar if they set it down overnight. Have them record their prediction. The next day, have partners observe their jar and record their observations. Discuss with the class the way the materials settled (i.e., they formed layers). Explain that when sediments are carried into lakes, rivers, and oceans, they settle to the bottom. These sediments are made up of different kinds of material. The larger, heavier materials settle first, and the lighter materials settle on top of the heavier layers. After a long time, the sediments sometimes harden into rock. These rocks are called sedimentary rocks. Discuss with the class how accurate their predictions were.

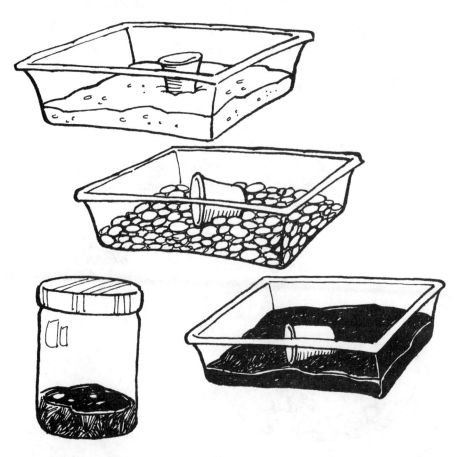

A Layered Paperweight

OBJECTIVE

● Students will build layers of different materials to understand how sedimentary rocks are formed.

MATERIALS

● 4 or more different-colored ingredients (e.g., rice, brown sugar, kidney beans, split peas)

● plastic spoons

● white glue

● picture of Grand Canyon (or other landform with sedimentary layers)

● baby food jars with lid (with labels removed)

In advance, place the ingredients, plastic spoons, and white glue at a table. Set a spoon next to each ingredient. Show the class a picture of the Grand Canyon or a different landform in which the sedimentary rock strata is clearly shown. Point out the layers of rock. Tell students that each layer is made up of different types of rocks. Explain that the oldest rocks are at the bottom and the youngest rocks are at the top. Have students determine that the layers are distinguished by color, texture, and composition. Tell students they will create a "layered paperweight" to help them understand how different types of sediment create different layers. Give each student a baby food jar. Have a few students at a time carefully spoon the ingredients into their jar to create alternating layers. When students have almost filled their jar to the top, have them put some glue along the top edge of the jar and screw on the lid securely. Have students set their jar aside until the glue is dry. Discuss with students how their ingredients are similar to sedimentary rocks. Invite students to display their paperweight for the whole class to admire.

- 2 types of bread
- waxed paper
- heavy books
- toaster oven

A Metamorphic Sandwich

OBJECTIVE

- Students will observe how heat and pressure can make an object harder and more compact.

Place three slices of bread on top of each other, making sure to have a different type of bread in the center. Place the bread between two sheets of waxed paper. Ask students what they think will happen to the bread if something heavy presses down on it. Record predictions on the board. Check the predictions by laying three or four heavy books on the bread. Wait 10 minutes, and then remove the books. Students will observe that the layers of bread have become thinner. Explain that the weight of the books made the layers of bread compressed (squeezed closer together). Next, place a slice of bread in a toaster oven. Ask students what will happen when the bread is toasted. Record student predictions on the board. Check their predictions by toasting the bread. Students will see that the heat from the toaster made the bread harder. Explain that just like the bread, rocks can be changed by heat and pressure. The properties and appearance of the rocks change. These changed rocks are called metamorphic rocks. Metamorphic rock is harder than the rock it comes from. Invite students to work with a partner and determine what other types of items could be used to give a visual of metamorphic rocks. Invite partners to share their visual with the class.

Investigating Sand

OBJECTIVE

● Students will observe grains of sand and see how they vary.

MATERIALS

● sand

● container (e.g., a medium-sized bowl or a pail)

● small paper plates

● plastic spoons

● magnifying glasses

● 3" (7.5 cm) black paper squares

● tweezers

● glue

● resealable plastic bags (optional)

Pour some sand into a container, and pass it around the classroom. Ask students where they think sand comes from. Explain that sand is made up of tiny pieces of rocks or minerals. Each piece is called a grain. Most grains of sand were once parts of larger rocks that crumbled away. Give each student a small paper plate, a plastic spoon, and a magnifying glass. Have students place a spoonful of sand on their plate. Then, have them use the magnifying glasses to observe that different minerals make up the sand. Have volunteers share their observations. Record student responses on the board. Students will see that the grains vary in size, shape, and color. Next, give each student a black paper square and tweezers. Have students use the tweezers to separate the grains according to size, shape, or color. Then, demonstrate for students how to glue similar grains together on the square. Have students place a drop of glue in one section of the paper and sprinkle, press, or drop the grains onto the glue. Display the paper squares on a table so that the class can compare the various groupings. To extend the activity, ask volunteers to help you collect samples of different varieties of sand from a beach, a playground, a park, a building supply store, or other places. Place the different kinds of sand in resealable plastic bags. Label each bag with the location the sand was taken from. Have students examine the samples with magnifying glasses to see how the grains of sand vary.

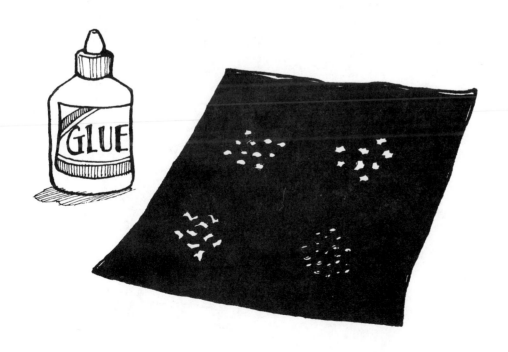

Fossil Imprints

MATERIALS

- pictures of prehistoric life
- picture of a fossil
- clean empty milk cartons with top flaps removed
- petroleum jelly
- shells
- sand
- water
- tub
- plaster of Paris

OBJECTIVES

Students will
- learn how fossil imprints were formed.
- make their own fossils.

Show the class pictures of prehistoric life. Ask students how scientists learn about life long ago. Show a picture of a fossil. Tell the class that one way scientists learn about prehistoric times is by studying fossils. Explain that fossils are the remains of plants and animals that lived long ago. These remains have been preserved in rock form. Scientists study fossils to understand what prehistoric plants and animals looked like. Tell students that in some fossils, the outlines of plants and animals are visible. Explain that these fossils formed when thin plant or animal parts were buried in sediment. The plant or animal parts then decayed. After the sediment turned to stone, only the outlines remained. These kinds of fossils are called *imprints* or *prints.* Tell students that they will be making their own "fossil." Give each student a milk carton, petroleum jelly, and a shell. Have students rub petroleum jelly over the surface of the shell while you mix sand and some water in a tub. The sand should be moist so it clumps together. Put some moistened sand in each milk carton. Have students pat the sand flat and smooth in the bottom of the carton. Ask them to press the shell in the sand to make an impression and then remove it. Have students smooth over the sand and start again if they make a mistake. While they are preparing their impressions, mix the plaster of Paris. Add enough water so the mixture is the consistency of pancake batter. Pour enough plaster into each milk carton to cover the impression. Let it harden. Later, have students peel off the milk carton and remove the sand. They will be left with a plaster impression of their shell.

Mold and Cast Fossils

MATERIALS

- gelatin mold
- fruit-flavored gelatin
- medium-sized bowl
- large spoon
- chopped fruits
- small paper plates
- spoons

OBJECTIVE

- Students will learn about how mold fossils and cast fossils were formed.

Show the class an empty gelatin mold, and have students identify what it is. Ask what would happen if you prepared a gelatin mixture, poured it into the mold, and then let the gelatin set in the refrigerator. Guide students to see that the gelatin would harden into the shape of the mold. Tell the class that some fossils formed in much the same way as gelatin forms in a mold. Explain that when the remains of a prehistoric plant or animal were buried in sediment, the sediment hardened to rock over time. The plant or animal parts then decayed. A hollow space in the rock—shaped like the original plant or animal—remained. This type of fossil is called a *mold fossil.* Explain that it is similar to the empty gelatin mold. Sometimes, dissolved minerals or other tiny particles filled the mold and then hardened. This resulted in a rock that had the exact shape of the original plant or animal. This type of fossil is called a *cast fossil.* It is similar to gelatin that has set in a mold. As a class, make "cast fossils" by preparing gelatin as directed on the package, and pour it into a mold. Add chopped fruits to represent the different particles or minerals that fill the mold. Chill the gelatin, and then invite students to taste the tasty treat.

Name_____ Date_____

Rock Colors

Directions: Check off the colors you see in each rock.

	Rock 1	Rock 2	Rock 3	Rock 4	Rock 5
black					
blue					
brown					
gray					
green					
orange					
pink					
purple					
red					
white					
yellow					

1 How many of your rocks were made up of only one color? _____

2 How many of your rocks were made up of more than one color? _____

3 The different colors in a rock show the different minerals in it. Look at your rocks. Are most rocks made up of one mineral or more than one mineral?

_____

Rocks and Minerals © 2003 Creative Teaching Press

Names_____ Date_____

Hardness Test

Directions: Draw your three rocks and color the pictures.

Rock 1   Rock 2   Rock 3

Scratch each rock with a fingernail and a nail. Each time you scratch, wipe the rock with a damp paper towel. Was a mark left on the rock? Write "yes" or "no" on the chart.

	Fingernail	Nail
Rock 1		
Rock 2		
Rock 3		

Which rock is the hardest? Which rock is the softest? How do you know?

_____

_____

_____

Layers of Sediment

Directions: Complete the activity to find out what happens to sediments in water. Record your predictions and findings.

Predict what will happen to the sand, gravel, and soil when you shake the jar.

_____

_____

Predict what will happen to the sand, gravel, and soil after it sits overnight.

_____

_____

_____

_____

Draw a picture in the box of what the materials in the jar looked like the next day.

Why do you think the materials looked the way they did? _____

_____

_____

Rocks at Work

OBJECTIVE

● Students will make a display that shows the different ways that people use rocks.

MATERIALS

● pictures of things made from rocks (e.g., buildings, bridges, sculptures, jewelry, mosaics)

● magazines, catalogs, and newspapers

● construction paper

● scissors

● glue

Show the class pictures of various things that have been made from rocks. Discuss the fact that rocks are used for making many functional things, such as roads and buildings, as well as objects of beauty, like sculptures and jewelry. Have students identify the pictures and then brainstorm other things that are made from rocks. Divide the class into pairs. Give each pair of students a magazine, catalog, or newspaper and a piece of construction paper. Have students cut out pictures that show the different ways people "put rocks to work." Have students glue their pictures on their paper and title their collage *Rocks at Work.*

ROCKS at WORK
by Jake and Amber

Murals of Workers

- pictures of people working with rock
- chart paper
- butcher paper
- crayons or markers
- library books, magazines, or resource material

OBJECTIVE

- Students will describe the ways in which rocks provide occupations for people.

Show the class pictures of people working with rock, such as workers paving a road, a sculptor carving a block of marble, or miners working in a coal mine. Discuss how rocks are used to produce numerous goods and services. Then, brainstorm with the class a list of occupations in which people work with rock. Record student suggestions on a piece of chart paper. The list might include bricklayer, construction worker, geologist, landscaper, mason, miner, paleontologist, potter, roofer, or sculptor. Divide the class into small groups. Give each group a piece of butcher paper. Invite groups to design a scene that shows people working with rock. For example, one group might illustrate a town in which a road is being paved, a brick wall is being built, and a stone walkway is being laid. Another group might show an art studio in which a potter is throwing clay on a wheel or a sculptor is creating a marble statue. Provide library books, magazines, and other resource materials that will help students conceptualize their scenes. Have groups share their completed mural with the class.

A Miniature Garden

OBJECTIVE

● Students will observe how rocks are used to beautify gardens.

Discuss how landscapers use rocks to create beautiful, picturesque gardens. Show the class pictures of such gardens from magazines or calendars. Explain that some gardens use rocks to border a particular area, such as a flower bed or walkway. Other gardens, called rock gardens, are designed with the ground almost entirely covered by rock. In these gardens, plants grow in small areas of soil among the rocks. Tell students that they will be designing miniature "gardens." Give each student garden materials, a small plastic plate, a plastic spoon, some modeling clay, and a container of soil or sand. Also, give students a paintbrush and a bowl filled with a mixture of equal parts glue and water. Have students use the paintbrush to spread a thick layer of the glue-and-water mixture on the plate. Tell them to use the spoon to sprinkle soil or sand over their plate to cover the bottom of it. Have students stand over a trashcan, turn their plate over, and carefully shake out the excess soil or sand. Then, have them use white glue to place other materials in their garden. For example, students might use pebbles to make "flower beds," "walkways," or other decorative features. Explain to students that in order to make twigs and other plants stand up in their garden, they should insert them into some modeling clay and then add glue to the base of the clay. Then, have students press the clay onto the plate. Invite students to share their completed garden with the class.

MATERIALS

● pictures of landscaped gardens that include rocks

● garden materials (e.g., twigs, dried or artificial flowers, leaves, pebbles)

● small plastic plates

● plastic spoons

● modeling clay (brown or green)

● small containers of soil or sand

● paintbrush

● mixture of equal parts white glue and water

● white glue

● bowls

- large index cards
- reference materials (e.g., library books, encyclopedias)
- colored pencils, crayons, and markers
- world map
- yarn

Famous Rock Formations

OBJECTIVES

Students will
- research a famous rock formation.
- find the location of the rock formation on a map.

Divide the class into pairs. Assign each pair an interesting rock formation from the list below to research. Give each pair of students an index card. Provide reference materials for students to use. Have students write on their index card a brief description of their chosen formation, including where it is located and the types of rocks from which it originated. Have partners also draw on their card a picture of their rock formation. Display a large world map in the center of a bulletin board. Invite each pair of students to locate on the map the country of their rock formation and share the information they learned about it with the class. Then, have students attach one end of a length of yarn to their index card and the other end to the corresponding place on the map. Staple the index cards around the map.

Famous Rock Formations
- Ayers Rock (Australia)—sandstone
- Carlsbad Caverns (New Mexico)—limestone
- Devils Postpile (United States)—basalt
- Dover Cliffs (England)—chalk, limestone
- Giant's Causeway (Northern Ireland)—basalt
- Grand Canyon (United States)—limestone, sandstone, shale, gneiss
- Great Sphinx (Egypt)—limestone
- Luray Caverns (United States)—limestone
- Monument Valley (United States)—sandstone
- Mount Rushmore (United States)—granite
- Natural Bridges (United States)—sandstone
- Pamukkale Falls (Turkey)—travertine
- Rainbow Bridge (United States)—sandstone
- Rock of Gibraltar (southern coast of Spain)—limestone
- Stone Mountain (United States)—granite

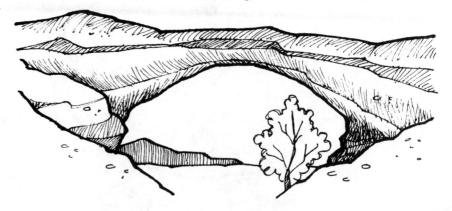

Sandpaintings

MATERIALS

- books on sandpainting such as *Indian Sandpainting of the Greater Southwest: Excerpts from Tapestries in Sand* by David Villasenor (Naturegraph)

- drawing paper

- circular, plastic lids (e.g., cottage cheese container lids)

- crayons

OBJECTIVE

- Students will learn about Navajo sandpaintings.

Share with the class a book about sandpainting. Explain to the class that the Navajo Indians of the Southwest are known for their sandpaintings. Explain that sandpainting is an ancient skill that is still practiced today. Each sandpainting is created for a certain purpose. One might be to ask for a good harvest. Another might be to help a person get well. Each sandpainting is made by pouring sand by hand onto the ground to make a design. Only five colors are used: yellow, black, red, blue, and white. Each color has a special meaning. To make a painting, they smoothed a small area of sand, and then they used their fingers to trickle different colors of sand onto the area. The designs were made from memory and were destroyed after the ceremonies. Explain to the class that most sandpaintings are somewhat symmetrical. This means that the painting could be divided in half and each half has elements that match the other. Display a sandpainting design. Invite volunteers to point out where a line of symmetry could be made on the design. Then ask students to identify those elements of the sandpainting that are symmetrical. Give each student a piece of drawing paper and a lid. Have students trace around the lid to make a circle. Tell students to use a pencil to draw a symmetrical design in the circle and use crayons to color it in. Invite volunteers to share their sandpainting and explain what their design represents.

What Makes a Hero?

OBJECTIVES

Students will
- learn about a hero from the past.
- distinguish what qualities make a hero.

Read *Return of Crazy Horse* to the class. Discuss how a Sioux chief inspired a sculptor named Korczak Ziolkowski to begin carving a mountain in his honor. Show students a picture of the Crazy Horse Memorial. Ask what kinds of qualities Crazy Horse had that inspired Ziolkowski to begin such an undertaking. For example, students might say *Crazy Horse stood up for what he believed in. He was a leader who fought hard for his people.* Ask students to pretend that they are artists who have been asked to paint or sculpt a work of art in honor of a hero. Have students write a paragraph explaining who they would choose and why. Tell students that the person does not have to be famous. For example, they may choose to write about someone from their family, school, or community. List the following questions on the board. Have students answer the questions in their writing.

- *What did the person do to make you think of him or her as a hero?*
- *What qualities do you admire in this person?*
- *Why would you want other people to learn about this person?*

Ask students to illustrate their writing. Invite volunteers to share their paragraph with the class.

A Game from Long Ago

MATERIALS

● rubber ball

● metal or plastic jacks

● 5 small pebbles (or rounded stones) for each pair of students

OBJECTIVE

● Students will learn about a pebble game that has existed for many years.

Show students a rubber ball and some jacks, and have them identify the objects. Ask students if they know how to play jacks, and demonstrate the game. With one hand, throw the jacks on the floor. Then toss the ball and, with the ball in the air, pick up one jack. Catch the ball after it has bounced once. Set the jack aside. Continue the procedure with the other jacks. Tell the class that various versions of jacks have existed all over the world for many years. The game was first played with small pebbles or stones. Tell students they will try playing jacks using pebbles. Divide the class into pairs. Give each pair five pebbles. Have partners take turns using one hand to throw four pebbles on the floor to begin round 1. Then, have the student toss the remaining pebble in the air. While it is in the air, have the student quickly pick up one of the four pebbles and catch the tossed pebble before it lands. Have the student continue tossing and picking up pebbles. Ask the partner to repeat the process. Then, have students throw the four pebbles on the floor to begin round 2. Tell students to play the same way as the first round but pick up two pebbles at a time. Then, have partners play the same way as the first and second round but pick up three pebbles on the first toss and the remaining pebble on the second toss. Finally, have students toss the remaining pebble in the air and pick up all four pebbles at once. Explain that whenever a player fails to pick up a pebble as described in the rules, his or her turn ends and the partner's turn begins. Whenever a player begins a new turn, he or she must start from the first round and go through all the steps again. The player to reach the fourth round first wins the game.

Name_____   Date_____

Rocks and Minerals Cumulative Test

Directions: Fill in the best answer for each question.

1 Which of these is **not** a type of rock?

- ⓐ marble
- ⓑ shale
- ⓒ chalk
- ⓓ calcite

2 What kind of rock forms from hardened lava?

- ⓐ igneous
- ⓑ sedimentary
- ⓒ metamorphic
- ⓓ mantle

3 Which of these words is a synonym for **molten**?

- ⓐ hard
- ⓑ melted
- ⓒ frozen
- ⓓ striped

4 What is the name of tiny pieces of rock that are carried by water into the ocean?

- ⓐ layers
- ⓑ fossils
- ⓒ magma
- ⓓ sediments

5 Which word is spelled correctly?

- ⓐ mineril
- ⓑ volcanoe
- ⓒ lava
- ⓓ corre

6 Rock A leaves a scratch mark on Rock B. What do you know about the rocks?

- ⓐ Rock A is a darker color than Rock B.
- ⓑ Rock A is softer than Rock B.
- ⓒ Rock B has less minerals than Rock A.
- ⓓ Rock A is harder than Rock B.

Rocks and Minerals Cumulative Test

7 What do scientists learn from studying fossils?

  ⓐ They learn how heavy rocks are.

  ⓑ They learn why rocks have different colors.

  ⓒ They learn what life was like long ago.

  ⓓ They learn which rocks are rare.

8 Pretend you saw a gem that was cut so that it had four sides. Which word describes its shape?

  ⓐ octagon

  ⓑ hexagon

  ⓒ pentagon

  ⓓ square

9 Pikes Peak is 4,110 feet (1,254 meters) high. Vesuvius volcano is 4,190 feet (1,278 meters) high. How much higher is Vesuvius than Pikes Peak?

  ⓐ 80 feet (24.4 meters)

  ⓑ 100 feet (30.5 meters)

  ⓒ 10 feet (3 meters)

  ⓓ 1,000 feet (305 meters)

10 The men who worked on the Mount Rushmore Memorial were paid $1.25 an hour. How much money would a worker earn in 4 hours?

  ⓐ $12.00

  ⓑ $5.00

  ⓒ $10.00

  ⓓ $4.00

11 Why do you think rocks are called an important natural resource?

_____

_____

12 What are two qualities a person should have in order to be a good geologist?

_____

_____

Certificate of Completion

Congratulations!

(Name)

Geologist in Training!

_____ (signed)

_____ (date)

Rocks and Minerals © 2003 Creative Teaching Press